Hugo da Luz

Meritocracy

Independent Edition

INDEX

Introduction..03

1. Democracy and Meritocracy...................................06

2. From low to high standards....................................12

3. Between Duties and Rights.....................................21

4. The Regime and the Society...................................25

Introduction

Meritocracy is a small philosophical and political essay that seeks to introduce us, in general lines, to the regime that is being constructed and defined, as its name says, on the top of an idea, or «the» idea, of *merit*.

To take our job forward throughout the text – but above all, initially –, we make a parallel with the regime that, for us, has the idea of *merit* in the antipodes of its nature and its identity (as a regime), i.e., democracy.

After, but in this same reasoning, we present the pros and cons of both socio-political systems, with the cons of democracy being presented as the result of its pros, as a consequence of its intrinsic contradictions.

And, on the top of these contradictions, i.e., aiming in theory the results that in practice this regime, by its very nature, will never be able to achieve, arises – as a result – Meritocracy, as the regime, *par excellence,* that, due to its nature and its own operating logic, presents more conditions to be able to embrace what democracy ingloriously can never achieve.

"There is no worse calamity in all human destiny than when the powerful of the earth are not, at the same time, the first among men. Then everything is deformed, everything becomes false and monstrous. (...) then the scum rises and takes value and the common virtue ends up saying: 'Look, only I am the virtue!'"

[Nietzsche, F. *Thus Spoke Zarathustra*]

Meritocracy

1. Democracy and Meritocracy

Meritocracy is a word that has not been used that often – not to say, a word almost unknown to most people – which, on the one hand, is negative, because it means that its value and utility are also unknown; but, on the other hand, it's positive, because it means that it's a word that, unlike many others, has not been vulgarized or lost importance.

Meritocracy is a word most commonly used in the Anglo-Saxon world, in particular, in countries like the United States or England. In these, it has markedly an entrepreneurial connotation, meaning that the *merit* is the quality of those who work the most, of those who work harder, of those who give more of themselves in their workplace; who, with this, most helps their company to increase the productivity and their boss to make more profits – which, recognizing their contribution, deservedly will increase their salary and even improve their hierarchical position in the company.

In these same countries these concepts of *merit* and *meritocracy* were adopted by Politics and Civil Society; meaning, first politically, the possibility of introducing in democracy something that is even strange to this regime, that is, the different treatment of people (because democracy is based on the idea that people should be treated as the same); whereas, socially and culturally (that is, at the Civil Society level) it means that the citizen who does something for his community – more than just waiting for the community to do something for him – must be recognized and valued by his fellow citizens.

However, these concepts of *merit* and *meritocracy* have two major flaws, both in absolute terms and in relative terms. In absolute terms, in the way the concept of *merit* itself is thought; and, in relative terms, in the way intellectuals try to reconcile democracy specific way of function with the true nature of the idea of merit (which are inherently incompatible). Let's do it by steps.

On the one hand, in absolute terms, the Anglo-Saxon concept of *merit* presents a fundamental problem, a problem, I will even say, of identity, since it appears lame, that is, defined, from our point of view, only by one of its two foundations (which are, both, inherently natural). Namely: for the foundation that is usually designated, by the French speaking, as *engagement,* or in English, *commitment*, that is, for the dedication, for the effort, for the greater work; leaving aside, either due to intellectual incompetence or ideological sadism, its other foundation, that is, the foundation of ethics; a foundation that, without it, it's useless to bet a lot on hard work, on dedication, on a greatest effort, if, at the same time, there is no mutual respect between people, consideration, whether between those in different hierarchical positions, or between pairs (either in a work context or in a social context).

If those who work hard (working hard in their workplace or working hard to make their community better) don't have the deserved respect and recognition *i)* of their superiors and are ignored (and, with this, they start to feel discourage and even start to work less), or *ii)* have this recognition and rise in the hierarchical position, but use that extra power to proudly disrespect their colleagues hierarchically below them or *iii)* not using that extra power and that position to demean those who are hierarchically below them, but instead, be objectively envied and see their work being sabotaged daily by all those who, mediocre and vindictively, come together to destroy every people who are simply more cultured, more intelligent, more capable and competent than them, that extra effort, this greater dedication, that more capable and intelligent way that would justify a promotion, it will be useless.

And therefore, whether is in the community or in the workplace, the effort, the commitment, the dedication (call it what you want), is something unquestionably positive. But, not alone; or because, without the other foundation, as I already mentioned, it is an impoverished, counterproductive and even problematic concept; or because, when accompanied by its other foundation and complete, it is a more enriching, progressive and resolving concept. Effort, dedication, commitment (call it what you want) and ethics must be the two foundations that define the concept of *merit* and, certainly, on the top of which a *meritocracy* must be built.

Now, meritocracy cannot be carelessly fused with democracy, because the nature of one and the nature of the other are not only different, but they are irreconcilable and irremediably incompatible! Let us, now, move on to the second part of our critique of the Anglo-Saxon concept of *merit* (in its relative sense).

In relative terms, the Anglo-Saxon concept of *merit* contains a disruptive contradiction, when it tries to live peacefully with the idea diametrically opposed to its basic idea: namely, the democratic idea of a dictatorially manufactured horizontalization of society (as opposed to the meritocratic idea of a naturally fair verticalization of society). Democracy and meritocracy have different ways of thinking; democracy and meritocracy have different principles and ends, as well as the means to get there; democracy and meritocracy are based on values that are nothing compared (they even excluded each another). Why, then, seek to give democracy another credibility (which it clearly does not have) by introducing in it the credibility that meritocracy definitely lends it? Why do they not let democracy take its course (for those who believe in it)? And instead of making meritocratic logic a kind of crutch for democracy, let democracy be left to its own destine (which, due to its idiosyncratic contradictions, we all know what is, for centuries) and, for those who believe, like me, in the meritocracy logic, a regime should be constructed, a new regime – the meritocratic regime – and, with it, we should search for what democracy contradictorily fails to achieve: *Progress*.

Based on the concept of *merit*, defined not by the entrepreneurial logic of devotion, without guarantees of recognition, without guarantees of mutual respect and without guarantees of a better life; but defined *i)* by logics of balance between what is dedicatedly done and what is proportionally obtained in exchange, both in terms of the wage value (you earn by what you proportionately do) and in terms of the hierarchical responsibilities (taking on positions on a scale of what we can do), *ii)* in terms of respect for and from the pairs, in and outside the workplace (respecting and being respected, regardless of the place in the hierarchy in which we find ourselves) or *iii)* in terms of these gains not only be translated into a better salary or a hierarchic promotion, but also in terms of a better quality of life[1].

---

[1] Personified in the maxim, 'to work hard, it is not to work well'; working a lot, many times, is even counterproductive, because, having more time to live, with a greater psychic and psychological degree associated with it, reflected later in the workplace, translates into a better and less sad effort and, with it, a better quality of work and a greater productivity.

2. From low to high standards

First, we looked at the concept of *merit* operating in some of the Western societies (i.e., in the Anglo-Saxon ones) and we presented their contradictions, both in absolute terms – in terms of the concept – and in relative terms – regarding the impossibility of meritocracy be only and contradictorily a kind of an appendix to the democratic regime.

Then, we talked about our concept of *merit* and the necessity to build a new regime, the meritocracy – built on a concept of *merit*, defined not only by the idea of an *engagement*, that is, by dedication, by commitment, by a greater work, but also by ethics, that is, by mutual respect between people, either in a work context, in a political context or in a civil context.

Now, it's up to us to present a general idea of the meritocratic regime, as opposed to the democratic regime, clarifying the differences and even the incompatibilities between one regime and the other; as well as evaluate the pros and cons of both, explaining why meritocracy is, in our perspective, more capable of dealing with the challenges and the problems that humanity has to deal with.

As its name implies, *meritocracy* is the regime where *merit*, that is, (what has) value, appears as its most relevant brand; as opposed to democracy, whose things and people, regardless of merit, i.e., regardless of their value, are still valued – a contradiction that Western societies are paying dearly[2].

To say that meritocracy is governed by merit, that is, by what has value, and democracy is not governed by merit, is the same as saying that in meritocracy people's behaviours, regardless of the social background to which they belong, regardless of their skin colour, regardless if they are men or women, regardless if they are young or old, they all must be governed by high standards of demand, that is, they must be governed by true values[3]; whereas in democracy happens diametrically the

---

[2] "Nothing in democracy, not coincidentally, 'separates the wheat from the chaff', that is, discriminates positive and constructively and it distinguishes what has quality from what has no quality; on the contrary, ideologically it discriminates negative and prejudicially the concept of 'discrimination' itself, adjectivizing it contradictorily with the same adjectives that characterize the accusation of those who adjectives it, forgetting that one can discriminate positive and constructively and that one can discriminate negative and prejudicially and these two things are totally different realities; and by putting them intentionally and ideologically in the same bag, not only what has quality is ignored and is not exemplarily promoted, but what has no quality is not disapproved and, in many cases, fair and constructively censored or even banned; allowing retrogradely that what has no value is, in most cases, seen as an example to follow – and this is what is on the table in our times." [Luz, H., *Music Today*, Independent Edition, pp. 51-52].

[3] People with merit, i.e., people with value, are people who, guiding their

opposite[4], that is, people, rich or poor, white or black, men or women, young or old, govern their behaviours by low standards of demand, that is, without any concern with the results of their actions and whether these, in any moment, may be harming others, and including themselves.

In democracy – as we understood – reigns the maxim, "anything works/is fine", in the music that is heard, in the cinema that is seen, in the art (in general) that is made, in the choice of the politicians that are elected, in the television programs that are seen, in the people with whom most human beings are accompanied, in the way we tolerate the bad services that are provided to us (the public and the private ones), etc. In other words, reigns the "culture" of the laxity, of the permissiveness, of the carelessness and of the sloppiness, i.e., reigns the "culture" of the Law of less effort, of the shortcuts, of "the easier (and faster) the better"[5] or, in other words, reigns the

---

behaviour by high standards of demand, that is, by high values, either professionally or ethically – i.e., never guiding their behaviour by false values – would be those who would almost certainly deserve the Plato's exceptional title of *philosopher's kings*; or would perfectly fit Nietzsche's extraordinary definition of *Supermen*.

[4] And it's for this reason that, for so many years, we heard people talking about a 'crisis of values' or a 'degeneracy of democracy' or even a 'regime's crisis' – the victim itself of its own contradictions and idiosyncrasies.

pseudoculture of the low standards of demand (with ourselves and, by contagious transmission, with the others).

However, this has a price! We cannot want to base our lives on the "Law of the less effort", speaking individually or collectively, and then hope that everything goes well, that is, that our lives improve and that our society progresses – in other words, that we can have a stronger economy, paying better salaries, that our artists can make better music, produce better cinema, present better art, than the one they have presented, that our politicians can be more competent and honest than what they have shown, that the Media respects their own code of ethics and be more impartial and pedagogical, that our schools can teach better and that our parents can truly educate their children, and can exist, with that, more cultured and civilized citizens, than the ones we unfortunately have.

---

[5] The epithet of the pseudoculture of *fast food*, which has spread far beyond gastronomy, and which has invaded other areas of societies; although – being honest – it has been influenced itself by the economic model imposed by *Savage Capitalism*, based on the idea of, «the greatest possible profit, with the least possible number of investments», in its turn influenced by the maxim of Modern Science, of the «best possible result , with the least possible effort employed» (the heart of the central concept of Modern thought, i.e., *efficiency*).

Both things are simply not compatible! To govern our lives, the individual ones and the collective, based on low standards of demand and, at the same time, hope that everything goes well – when we know that, for things to go well, it requires work, dedication, effort and ethical values – that is simply not possible!

What has quality and value takes work! Regardless of if we are talking about things or people. It does not appear overnight or with a simple snap of fingers. It takes time! It takes its time. It does not fall from the sky, nor does it appear without any work and dedication, as if it were a kind of a miracle.

For a human being to have value and add quality to everything he does, it takes time. Every child needs values, needs to be accompanied and adequately nurtured, needs to be surgically corrected and held accountable, needs good examples and knowledge, etc. We can't expect much from a child, in a few years, if his parents didn't take any responsibility for his education: if they didn't follow this child, giving him everything he needs and making him progressively responsible, throughout his growing years, for everything that he did; but instead, having given him the possibility to adopt a thoughtless behaviour, whenever he did something wrong, not calling him to reason, in order to assume the responsibility for his own acts.

Music, cinema, in one word, art (with quality, of course) is not for everyone! – contrarily to what was and continues to be said by the gurus of democracy. It's not just because you want to, but because you've worked over several years to make it happen – It's not just because you grab a microphone and go up on stage, or you grab a camera or a brush and a painting canvas, that suddenly you become an artist. Valuable things take work and talent. Even if this is an invisible work, like the work of art.

And it's not in this democratic "culture" of the easiness, of the permissiveness, of the false illusions, of the infantilism, of the hyper-tolerance, of the irresponsibility, of the self-excuses, which always degenerates into a "culture" of the proudly mediocre, the proudly bad, ill-educated and incorrect, of the proudly ignorant, the proudly marginal and the proudly ugly[6], that we will, of course, be able to get the best out of the human beings – be it in the music they create, in the cinema they make, or in the exemplary posture with which they are in society, in relation to others, etc.

---

[6] This pseudoculture, which was very influenced initially by the tribal counterculture of the proud "*ugly, dirty and bad*", which did not have an immediate and significant impact on societies at that time, ended up making its way.

An education based on low standards of demand means that we are bringing out not the best of the human beings, but their worst – meaning, in a large scale, to fail in the possibility of having a better society and a better world. The opposite is also true. An education based on high standards of demand, around which we guide our behaviours, means that we are bringing out the best of the human being, the best music, the best cinema, the best art, the best decisions (political decisions and other kind of decisions), the best citizenship, the best attitudes, the best ideas, in just a few words, the best that a human being can give, that is, the quality and the value to everything a human being does, regardless if he's doing politics, music, painting, cinema, journalism or other things.

This greater demand, this education, this true education, based on high standards of demand, we cannot expect it to come from democracy, because it's not in its DNA. This greater demand, this greater value, as a result of this education, based on high standards of demand, only meritocracy, by its true nature, can provide.

People cannot base their lives on low standards of demand and then hope to achieve positive results! They cannot continually base their behaviours on low standards of self-demand and hope that their lives will get better. People cannot demand nothing from themselves, but demand everything from others, and hope that someday they will succeed – because that doesn't happen. People cannot educate a child or an adolescent basing that education on low standards of demand and then think that it's possible to get the best out of that child or that teenager – because that is impossible.

And therefore – translating meritocracy into practice –, people cannot have no values or no education and have power in their hands (as that power democracy indiscriminately gave them). They cannot have no scruples and simultaneously have the moral authority to have a ballot paper on their hands. They cannot fail to fulfill their duties and continue to disproportionately demand more rights and more guarantees. They cannot have high standards of demand with others (specially with politicians) and low standards of demand with themselves. They cannot continue to criticize their bosses and Capitalism and spend their lives in their workplace pretending to do things or appearing to comply with the contract. They cannot lazily continue to envy those who strive in life (and, as a result, achieve better levels of quality in their life) and spend their lives on coffee terraces or hours and hours on Facebook, day after day, week after week, months and years in a row, entertained with useless and predictable conversations. People cannot attack teachers in schools or doctors in hospitals or attack law enforcement officials and do not see their rights being proportionately removed. People cannot continue to complain, expecting success to fall from the sky, wanting to have a better life than their neighbour, who contrary to them (for having a higher level of self-demand), instead of wasting time whining and envying others, works hard, year after year, becoming a much better person, more adapted to life and to its intrinsic obstacles.

Doing nothing, nothing happens! And to base our lives on low standards of self-demand means not demanding anything from ourselves; and not demanding anything from ourselves, always demanding everything from others (from our parents, from our friends, from the State, from God, from the husband, from our wife, from our grandparents, etc.), means believing that we can have everything, without doing nothing. But the question is: what if the others, from whom everything is requested, thought the same way, what society would we have?

3. Between Duties and Rights

There is and there was always a disproportionality between duties and rights over time.

It happened in the past and it still happens in the present. Before, speeches circled mainly around duties, to the detriment of rights; now, speeches rotate largely around rights, to the detriment of duties.

In the past, societies, whatever they were, from North to South, from East to West, were built more around the idea of citizens' duties and obligations, without a contraposition from the State to ensure the fulfillment of its own obligations, in the diametrical and umbilical respect for the rights of its fellow citizens – sliding this, for that reason, so often, in abuses and violations of the most basic rights of the people, translated into historical episodes, known to all, that have become almost the hallmark of the human History, Power and of the human nature itself, with its fragile and corruptible way of being, whenever is seduced.

Today this disproportionality between duties and rights happens, but in reverse. Democratic societies are also being built, as past societies were, based on this logic of disproportionality; however, now, instead of a disproportionate difference between rights and duties, where duties assume a relevant requirement, this disproportionality is guided more by a difference between rights and duties, where rights and their demand constitute a brand image, in which duties do not seem to represent any importance in the construction of a political framework, where the lucidity of the proportionality between rights and duties is the determining factor for the balance that has never been reached till today, either by conservative regimes or by reactionary regimes (such as that one we have in the West today, i.e., democracy).

Duties and rights do not exist alone. Duties and rights are umbilical and proportionally interconnected. When there are more duties than rights and vice-versa, there is automatically a disproportion and consequently an injustice; an injustice or because there are more duties than rights or an injustice because there are more rights than duties. Past societies have been unfair, because the balance has inclined more to one side than to the other; societies today are just as unfair, because, due to democracy, the balance falls more to the opposite side of the side to which it has previously fallen.

Injustices are injustices! It is not because the injustices of today are different from the unquestionable injustices from the past that it makes them less unjust. We cannot reactionarily fight injustices with (other) injustices. We cannot perpetually continue with past models and past logics, just reversing the roles (who was on the top, is now below and vice-versa) and think that we are changing something truly structural[7].

Anyone, rich or poor, white or black, male or female, western or eastern, old or young, in a society that wants to be progressive, just cannot have more duties than rights or more rights than duties! And, in this logic, people, whoever they are, can only be asked to fulfill their duties in the exact proportion of seeing their rights secured, that is, they can only comply with their obligations, if the State has already fulfilled its duties; and, on the other hand, but in the same logic, they can only see their rights guaranteed in the exact proportion of having previously fulfilled their duties.

---

[7] As it happens today, under the influence of Postmodernism and, more specifically, under the influence of Post-Postmodernism, and the 'moral of resentment and revenge' (predicted by Nietzsche), that this movement (against Tradition and past models) originated; in particular, with the ironically sexist and racist narrative of the 'History of the White Man' (and well succeed), that pretends, in practice, not to combat sexism and racism, with an agenda for gender *equality* and for the *equality* between different peoples, but pretends, above all, to combat chauvinism, by instigating sexist behaviour in women against men (as if men, just because they are men, were all bad) and to combat white racism by instigating racist behaviour in all peoples against whites (in particular, against white men), as if being white was in itself a defect.

And, therefore, in a situation in which the State does not fulfill its duties, the citizen who was directly neglected by this unfulfillment should not have the obligation to proportionally fulfill his (duties); just as, inversely, when a citizen does not fulfill his obligations, the State, at a pedagogical title, must also, in the same proportion, not guarantee the rights umbilical and intrinsically associated with those duties not fulfilled by that particular citizen.

4. The regime and the Society

It is in this continuation, of a historical disproportionality between duties and rights, however now — with democracy — disproportionately more inclined towards the side of rights, to the detriment of duties, that we analyse the consequences of this injustice, in particular, the consequences of taking to exaggeration this idea of inclining speeches and behaviours childishly more to the side of rights, with the irresponsible disregard of the fulfillment of duties, in terms of the construction or the destruction of a society.

We must not live in society, as if we lived outside of it! — that is, as savages or as uncivilized creatures. In the same way, we don't expect from anyone who lives outside society, to live as if he was living inside of it (which would be absurd)[8].

---

[8] Living — as modern jusnaturalists defended — in a *civil state* would imply respecting the *Social Contract* signed between, on the one hand, the Civil Society, i.e., the people and, on the other hand, their representatives, i.e., Power, giving people up part of their *natural state*, i.e., of their natural freedom, that is, of their savage and animal way of being (the way human beings relate to each other, without any mediation by the State, through the Law and its norms), with the guarantee of people gaining in exchange something that this *natural state* (this natural coexistence, this community without Law) cannot guarantee, i.e., life, the subsistence and security of

We must live in society as someone who behaves like someone who lives in society, that is, in a civilized way; in the same way, it is expected that someone who lives outside society behaves like someone who lives outside society, that is, in a wild or uncivilized way.

Now, we cannot have an inversion of this logic, and with this seriousness, and think that we do not live in a great asylum, as Nietzsche considered to be the dystopia in which democracy would inevitably degenerate, due to its own idiosyncratic nature – which even led him to affirm, in his *Zarathustra*, that it was more dangerous to live among men than among animals and, for this reason, societies had themselves become more like a jungle than a true society.[9] (in the technical and philosophical sense of the word).

---

human beings, with which this agreement was celebrated. That the *Social Contract* was long ago visible and unquestionably abandoned by the representatives of the Civil Society (that is, by the *Single Will*, by the Power), we all know that. Now, to be the Civil Society itself, the people, to abandon this agreement, it only shows the level of degeneration of the society and the eventual need to make a new *Social Contract* – correcting what was done wrong, keeping what was done correctly and add new nuances to this new agreement, betting on a contract based, this time, in the meritocracy molds.

[9] "O loneliness! O my homeland loneliness! (...) O Zarathustra, I know everything; and I know that in the crowd you felt more abandoned (...) I found more danger among men than among animals – that was abandonment!"

We cannot live in society as if we lived outside it, that is, in an uncivilized and even wild way; since we don't expect anyone who lives outside society, to live as if they were living within it. And, therefore, I am not waiting for someone who lives outside society, to follow the rules, to be polite, to be civilized, to do no noise to his neighbours, etc. But I'm already waiting that someone who lives within a society to do it so – for the simple fact of living within it. Otherwise, we are witnessing a degeneration of society itself – and therefore, it's necessary to do something urgent, so this situation can be reversed.

We cannot live with one foot inside society and the other foot outside society! We cannot have one of our feet inside society's territory, when society has something we want; and have the other of our feet outside society's territory, when society has something we don't want – things don't work that way (or perhaps they do, but for childish or confused minds). We cannot live with one foot inside society, when it comes to claim our rights and, at the same time, live with the other foot outside society, when it comes to fulfill our duties – as it happens, indeed, and in a systemic way, in democracy.

When we choose a path, we commit to take it (to the end) and accept all its good and bad aspects. All choices in life have

---

[Nietzsche, F. *Thus Spoke Zarathustra*, Europe-America, p. 180].

their pros and cons, their roses and their thorns. Now, there are choices with more pros than cons and other choices with more cons than pros. And living in society, specifically, was the choice that human beings made (thousands of years ago), knowing that this choice has cons, thorns, duties; but, despite that, compared to the pros of living in society and compared to the cons of living outside it, those cons of living in society were definitely minor – and the only thing we would have to do, no matter how much it cost (and it costs), was to fulfill our duties.[10]

If in past societies all obligations were required from people, without any right being recognized (no matter how basic it was); today, in societies where democracy is implanted, the situation is no better, in terms of a fair proportionality between duties and

---

[10] "Everything in life has its pros and cons! However, there are things in life that have more pros than cons and there are things that have more cons than pros. But nothing in life has only pros or cons – only good things or only bad things. That doesn't exist! The right philosophy of life is to understand exactly what has more pros than cons and choose that path, without ever forgetting that, however, we are embarking on a path that, despite having more pros than cons, that doesn't invalidate that this path doesn't have cons. In the same way, the same philosophy teaches to realize that what has more cons than pros has also pros, that is, that the fact of having more cons than pros, that doesn't invalidate of having pros." [Luz, H., *Fragments of a Wanderer's Diary*, Independent Edition, p. 28].

rights; if before everything was required from people and nothing was given to them in return, in today's societies everything is given to them, nothing or little is required from them (in comparison with what is given to them) and, apparently, nothing (of everything that is given to them) seems to be sufficient.

This disproportionality between duties and rights, if in the past has created a lot of injustices, due to the imbalance that has existed between what was demanded and what was given in return (reaching situations of extreme abuse), today this disproportionality between duties and rights, with a greater inclination for rights and an almost total dismissal of the proportional fulfillment of duties, has created a "culture" in which (as a result of the automatic infantilization and mediocrization created by it) everyone, no matter how many rights they have, these never seem to be enough; and when it comes to fulfill their duties, not only nobody wants to fulfill them; when, as a result, someone else's rights are not respected (as a result of someone not having fulfilled their duties), nobody seems interested in assume their responsibilities, their mistake, and grow with it.

Never before has the influence of *Enlightenment* thinking been so necessary in our Western societies! The infantilization and mediocrization carried out by democracy (for the reason given above) is destroying not only democracy itself, but it's even destroying society[11]. Democracy is rapidly degenerating – although, there are those who try not to believe it. But it is in accelerated degeneration (or, in one word, in *crisis*), for its own fault and not for others fault, for example, for Capitalism fault – as many manipulators want to make us believe, since the most solid democracies, like it or not, are found in countries where Capitalism is stronger; whereas in countries where there is a strongest resistance to Capitalism, there is no democracy, but extreme-Left dictatorships, such as North Korea, Cuba, Venezuela, China, etc.

And it's in crisis for its own fault, because, contrary to what they always say (i.e., Marx, Marxists and neo-Marxists), it's not

---

[11] "*Enlightenment* is man's emergence from his self-imposed nonage. Nonage is the inability to use one's own understanding without another's guidance. This nonage is self-imposed if its cause lies not in lack of understanding but in indecision and lack of courage to use one's own mind without another's guidance. *Sapere aude*! Dare to know! Have the courage to use your own understanding, is therefore the motto of the *enlightenment*. Laziness and cowardice are the reasons why such a large part of mankind gladly remain minors all their lives, long after nature has freed them from external guidance (*naturaliter maiorennes*). They are the reasons why it is so easy for others to set themselves up as guardians. It is so comfortable to be a minor." [Kant, I. *The Perpetual Peace*. Textos Filosóficos, Edições 70, Lisboa-Portugal, pp. 11-19].

only Capitalism that has the seed of its own self-destruction within itself; democracy also has it; in fact, all ideologies have it, be they political, economic, philosophical, scientific, religious, etc. – and even Marxism and neomarxism have this seed. Meaning this, that they are all fallible. And I'm not the one who says it. It was Socrates who said it, centuries and centuries ago, using other terminology, when he tried to teach his disciples to dismantle any thesis with which they disagreed and needed to refute it.[12].

But this seed of democracy's self-destruction, embodied in its contradictions, idiosyncrasies and in its low standards "culture", in the face of everything that our duties in society are concerned with, is not only destroying democracy itself; as a matter of fact, is destroying a much more important and ancestral project than the regime itself; we're referring to the project known by the name «society» and the idea of living in society, as opposed to the idea of living outside it – in other words, the only truly revolutionary idea and the only revolution to take place in the

---

[12] According to Socrates, to expose what Marx, with another terminology, considered to be the seed of the self-destruction of an ideology (in this specific case, of Capitalism), it would be necessary to take to the extreme the logic of the arguments which support a thesis, in order to wait for its contradictions to come out, and, in that moment, expose the thesis as illogical and impracticable.

history of mankind, i.e., Man deciding to stop living in the trees or in caves and start to live in communities, built on rules, norms and principles, which for centuries allowed humanity to self-subsist and perpetuate, until today.

These rules and basic principles of coexistence, more or less peaceful, between human beings, in a certain territory, more commonly known by the term "society", with these democracies and the aggravation of them being badly influenced by Post-Modernism or, more specifically, by Post-Postmodernism, it is proving to be totally disastrous, both for democracy itself, and above all for (the idea of living in) society.

Printed in Great Britain
by Amazon